1

Tax Tips for Authors

by a Writer and

Tax Professional

N. S. Smith

with EM Lynley

Published by Silk Road Press &
Rocky Ridge Books

ISBN: 978-1-62622-009-6

N.S. Smith & EM Lynley

Contents

Updated for 2013 Tax Returns

This January 2014 Third Edition contains all-new material and the most recent relevant tax-law changes, including the new simplified method of calculating the home-office deduction.

Smaller updates may occur between now and the 2015 Edition. If you would like to be informed of updated information, please consider subscribing to the Tax Tips for Authors Newsletter.

Introduction

This book is a compilation of lectures and additional information used in my online tax courses for authors in the United States. It is not intended to be an extensive or exhaustive volume on small-business taxes or general tax concepts. It's short, concise information that is of the most use to writers preparing their own tax returns. This book is not filled with lots of long-winded stories about clients to fill word count and add pages. You don't have time to read all that. You probably just want to know how to fill in your forms and what you can and can't deduct. I will answer those questions, as well as provide additional useful and necessary information.

Contact us at the blog: Tax Tips for Authors: (http://taxtips.emlynley.com or http://www.facebook.com/taxtipsforauthors)

Who is this book for?

Most writers, at least novelists, probably consider themselves left-brain types, more interested in words and ideas than in numbers and analytics. I happen to be an exception to that, starting out in science and engineering and moving into finance. (Physics and finance use the same math techniques). I've always been a numbers person and do freelance financial writing in addition to writing novels. I thought it would be useful to present some important tax issues from the perspective of a writer, for writers, using my own knowledge and experience as a financial professional and a tax preparer.

For those of you who do not know me, I write erotic romance, but during tax season I work as a tax preparer as well as for some private clients—mainly authors. I prepare my own taxes, including those for my writing business, and have been doing so since before I took a basic tax class at H&R Block. I am licensed in the state of California, which allows me to work as a paid tax preparer in California, though I can file any federal tax return and returns for nearly any state.

Since writers usually don't enjoy preparing their taxes, we tend to put off even thinking about them until the last minute. While you have until April 17 this year, due to a holiday, it's a good idea to think about your writing business from a tax perspective all year long, especially in regard to keeping track of what you spent. It also makes preparing your taxes a snap when all the information is readily available.

This book will cover mainly federal tax issues for two reasons:

> 1.   the majority of states use the federal adjusted gross income (AGI) from your 1040 as

the starting point, so deductions allowed at the federal level carry through to the state tax return; and

2.   I do not have detailed knowledge about other states besides California. If you have a specific state-related question, I can steer you in the direction of an answer, but I won't claim to be an expert about your state.

Can't I just do this myself?

Why do I need to read your book or take one of your courses? My software will do this all for me.

This is the biggest question I get when I prepare taxes for clients. Invariably, they tell me I asked more questions and found more deductions for them than they would have on their own. I will let you know that having a tax professional prepare your 1040 with Schedule C can run around $400, depending on the type of expenses you claim.

You certainly can do it yourself with tax software, but after you read this book, you'll have a lot more knowledge about what you can and cannot deduct, and why the software is asking some of those questions. You may also discover a few things you didn't know you could write off, which will help you lower your taxes, or avoid making costly mistakes that can trigger an audit.

Important Disclaimer

While I am licensed in California and bonded, this book is not intended to be the sole source of information in preparing your taxes, nor does it imply a client relationship between myself and any reader.

The information contained in this book is provided for informational purposes only, and should not be construed as legal advice on any subject matter. No recipients of content from this site, clients or otherwise, should act or refrain from acting on the basis of any content included in the site without taking into account or seeking appropriate tax advice on the particular facts and circumstances at issue for their financial situation. This book contains general information and may not reflect current legal developments, verdicts or settlements.

TO ENSURE COMPLIANCE WITH INTERNAL REVENUE SERVICE CIRCULAR 230, ANY U.S. FEDERAL TAX ADVICE CONTAINED IN THIS BOOK IS NOT INTENDED OR WRITTEN TO BE USED, AND CANNOT BE USED, FOR THE PURPOSE OF (1) AVOIDING PENALTIES UNDER THE INTERNAL REVENUE CODE OR (2) PROMOTING, MARKETING OR RECOMMENDING TO ANOTHER PARTY ANY TAX-RELATED MATTER[S] ADDRESSED HEREIN.

Chapter 1: General Legal Issues

What licenses, registrations or fees must you pay? Do you need to incorporate? Do you need an Employer ID number (EIN)?

There are no federal requirements for licensing a business, but your state may have specific rules and regulations. You can research your own state by visiting their website. Most states websites have a section for small businesses. You can find it by Googling the name of your state and "small business license" and the results should set you on the right path.

While I haven't looked into every state, the most likely registration or license you will need is if you sell books (electronic or physical) directly to readers who live in your state. You'll be required to apply for a sales tax permit and need to file monthly or quarterly reports of your sales, broken down into total sales and in-state sales, then remit the sales tax collected to the state entity. In California it's the California State Board of Equalization.

If you self-publish and sell only through distributors like Amazon, Barnes & Noble, Smashwords, and the like, they keep track of sales taxes since they are the seller, not you. But if you sell off your own website and you live in a state that collects sales tax, you'll need to ask each buyer what state they live in, collect tax from buyers only in your state, and send it on to the state.

If you are the sole owner of your business, you won't need to incorporate. If you own a writing or publishing business with someone else, including a spouse, consider incorporating to avoid legal and financial headaches down the road with your partner in case there are any difficulties or you want to shield your personal finances from creditors or lawsuits.

An Employer Identification Number or EIN is not required for a sole proprietorship, but if you incorporate you will need to apply for one from the Internal Revenue Service. The main reason you may want one is if you pay anyone else during the year for services, and need to issue a 1099-MISC. It's preferable to have an EIN rather than using your social security number, to avoid identity theft. It also makes you look more professional.

Here is more information on the IRS website regarding the EIN application process:

http://www.irs.gov/Businesses/Small-Businesses-&-Self-Employed/Apply-for-an-Employer-Identification-Number-(EIN)-Online

Chapter 2: Hobby vs. Business

Let's start off with a topic which is very important to the IRS.

Is your writing a hobby or a business?

Why does this matter? The IRS lets you deduct expenses on hobbies only up the amount of income, while if you write as a business, you can deduct all your expenses, even if it adds up to a loss. If you have other income (wages, retirement, lottery winnings, interest, dividend, etc.) you can lower your adjusted gross income and thus your taxable income, by using business losses to offset your "regular" earnings.

Here's an example:
Walter Writer works days as a dog groomer and earned $25,000.

He earned $1000 from sales of a self-published book on dog grooming.

He had $2000 of expenses from writing, publishing and promoting his book.

If Walter's writing is a hobby, he can only deduct expenses up to his writing earnings of $1,000. So his gross income is still $25,000. He doesn't have to report the hobby income unless he made a gain.

If Walter intends to keep writing, and trying to sell his books, he can call his writing a business. Maybe he'll break even in the second year of his endeavors. If Walter files his taxes, classifying his writing as for-profit, his tax situation looks like this:

$25,000 wages

($1,000) loss on writing business

= $24,000 adjusted gross income AGI (assuming no other adjustments to income)

That's a better situation, isn't it?

So it sounds simple, right? Let's just call it a business and write off everything! Not so fast. There are two reasons why you should seriously consider how to classify your writing.

Remember, you still have to report your hobby income, and it is taxable, but if you call yourself a business, you must show a profit in *three out of five years,* or the IRS may ask you for some proof you are running a real business and not just taking losses on what is really a hobby. More about this, called the "hobby-loss rule," later on.

Hobby writers: there is nothing wrong with writing as a hobby. It's great to have a little extra income to supplement your regular job or family income. For many writers, they see their own royalties as a way to pay for all those books they normally read. If you earn $500 this year as a writer, and you spent $500 on books in the same genre, you may be able to justify writing off a lot of the books as "research," and not have to claim any taxable income from writing.

Business writers: you can deduct everything related to starting and operating your writing business, even if you incur a loss. If writing is not your only business or you have regular wage income, this can reduce your taxable income, and allow you to pay lower taxes. The flip side is you have to file more forms as part of your tax return, and you will have to show some proof that you are attempting to make money as a business, even if you don't have a profit. The IRS expects a business to be profitable three out of five years, so if you have three years of losses in a row, chances are the IRS will tell you do to some 'splainin'.

The Hobby-Loss Rule

That's where the hobby-loss rule kicks in. If you show more years with losses than with profits at your "business," the IRS goes from assuming you're running a business to being very, very skeptical. They will flag your return and will ask to see several years of records that prove your intent to make a profit.

How to prove you are running a business

It's not difficult to show you are trying to run a profitable writing business. You don't need to do all of these, but even a few of the following activities will be enough to support a claim that you are running a business rather than indulging in a hobby:

> Get yourself a website and a domain name for your pen name or writing business name (all deductible)

> Participate on a regular basis in both writing and marketing your work.

> Take a class, online or in person, about writing and about the business of writing.

Establish a separate bank or PayPal account for your writing.

Keep records of everything that goes in or out of your business account and how it relates to your business

Make quarterly estimated tax payments (more on that later) in addition to any withholding from your wages

Write up a basic business plan, including writing schedules, target publishers, publication dates, marketing programs and activities

File Schedule C (Business Income) on your tax return

As you can see, if you are already published chances are you already doing many of these activities. What sets a business apart from a hobby is that you continue to do these activities on a regular basis, even after your first book is published. **You keep writing, keep marketing, and keep learning how to be a better writer, which includes how to make money at the *business* of writing.**

The IRS will also look at the distribution of your expenses. If you go to conferences, but don't do any promotion/advertising and don't have research expense or a new book coming out each year, they may wonder just what you are doing that is "business."

If you are writing, but getting rejection letters, then file those away as proof you tried. You aren't expected to be good at your business, but you are expected to try to make money, which means cutting back on expenses when you don't make money, and figuring out more ways to make money if what you did last year didn't work.

Remember, it's fine if you do see your writing as a hobby and don't want to go the extra distance to establish yourself as a business. But make sure to report your writing income as hobby income on Line 21 of Form 1040 when you file your taxes, rather than as a Schedule C business. You can deduct legitimate expenses up to the amount of the income as "Miscellaneous Deductions" on Schedule A. If you do not itemize, you will not be able to deduct your hobby expenses.

However, if you report large amounts of hobby income, the IRS might question the status, since businesses are subject to Self-Employment Tax, which we'll talk about later on. They will expect you to pay additional tax on that income at some point.

How about just not reporting the writing income and avoiding all that hassle and additional tax?

First off, I cannot recommend that you do this. I don't recommend that you do this.

In fact you may not be able to hide that writing income. If your publisher sends you a 1099-MISC form to report royalties or "non-employee compensation," it means the IRS got a copy too. So you can't just ignore that income when filing your taxes. If you made several thousand dollars on 1099's and don't report it, even if it all went to hobby expenses, that may also trigger a flag over at the IRS, and they may want to see what expenses you actually had. So, it's important to think this decision over and report all writing income on your taxes, and claim only reasonable expenses that contributed to business activities: making money.

Another important consideration, especially for those who make a significant portion of their income from writing is that unless you report the income and pay self-employment tax on it, you're not counted in the social security retirement system. If you get wages from a regular job, they withhold FICA—and it goes toward the big social security pool that you might want to tap into in your golden years. Your SE tax goes into that pool and entitles you to get more out of it later on. If you don't have other income you may never qualify for retirement benefits from social security.

So, it's important to think the hobby vs. business decision over and report all writing income on your taxes, and claim only reasonable expenses.

What's a reasonable expense? We'll get to that in a later lecture

When Do You Want Be Considered a Hobby?

There are times when it's best to be a hobby.

If you don't cover your expenses because you aren't putting in the hours writing on a regular basis, then I strongly suggest you classify yourself as a hobby. You won't have to pay SE tax on any profits, since it's not your livelihood, but you won't be able to take a loss either.

If the majority of your income is from W-2 wages and you are putting money into your retirement from your "day job." This saves you SE tax on profits, without compromising your future Social Security/retirement benefits.

Chapter 3: Recordkeeping Basics

Today is going to be a bit of a consolidation day before we get into the meat of the Schedule C. If you go through these assignments you will have a good start toward understanding the Expense section a little better, and you'll be able to target your reading and your questions once we start discussing those topics.

This will also help you set up a more efficient and useful system for keeping track of 2014 expenses before we get too far into the new year.

Assignment #1

What? No one told me there would be *homework!*

Relax. I won't know if you don't do the assignments, but you will be very glad you did.

Part 1

GOAL: Set up 2014 expense logs for easy recordkeeping

Go to the store tomorrow and buy one of those annual calendar planner things. The cheap kind with the plastic-y fake leather covers that have 2 pages per month work great for keeping track of expenses. Make sure it has a big box for each individual day. It's already 2014 so they are probably about $1 at Wal-mart or Target.

Even if you already have a calendar for your appointments, get another one for business use only, just to humor me. Don't use the one that has your kid's birthday and dog's teeth-cleaning appointments in it for the rest of the year. Get a special one for your writing, and prove your writing deserves its own special calendar. (That will also remind the IRS that you are running a business, because you have a calendar just for business expenses.)

If you have two different businesses (writing plus editing, formatting, cover art, promo company, etc.) I suggest getting a separate expense calendar/log for each one. You may end up combining on your tax return, but you should keep each business activity separate so you can monitor profitability, advertising, etc., to see what works best for each separate activity.

You may be a spreadsheet kind of person (not that many writers are in my experience, but just in case).It's fine to keep track of expenses on a spreadsheet too. Once we get to the section on types of expenses, you may find it useful to organize your spreadsheet by expense category, which will make adding everything easy when it comes time to file your tax return.

Part 2

GOAL: Become familiar with the different types of Schedule C expenses

Download a copy of the Schedule C from the IRS website:

http://www.irs.gov/pub/irs-pdf/f1040sc.pdf

Take a good look at Part II, Expenses.

Note the types of expenses listed. We will be going over every single line in this book, but it's going to help you a lot if you can start to think about each expense you have in terms of which line it belongs on. This simplifies your recordkeeping and reduces the time it takes to do your tax return.

If you are the spreadsheet type, consider having a worksheet (page in a spreadsheet, not separate spreadsheets) for each type of expense (combine a few if you find you don't have many of a particular kind), and then set up the spreadsheet to bring worksheet totals into one sheet in the same order as the Schedule C.

If you have started organizing for your 2013 tax return, pile up your receipts by line item.

Part 3
    GOAL: Start tracking expenses

Put down the last thing you spent money on for your writing. It was probably the price you paid for this book. So, go to your email and check when you ordered the book and write down on the calendar

    Tax Tips for Writers Book ($____ how much you spent for this book, unless you paid during 2013, then it should be on your 2013 expense sheet.)

(Actually, the cost of the calendar is likely the last thing you spent, so put that down, too).

At the end of every day (or week), collect up receipts or write down what you spent for your writing business that week, and **write it in the calendar**. Collect all the receipts in a special envelope you keep in the back of the calendar so you can find them again when you file your return, and then in the event the IRS starts asking questions. They tend to wait a year or three, so hold onto everything, organized by year.

If you write it down in the calendar on the day you spent it, you won't need to fiddle with all those receipts in April when you're freaking out about finishing Schedule C. It will become a good habit.

Here's what I wrote in my calendar recently. I went to the San Francisco Public Library to return some books for research and to get some more.

-   10 miles round trip drive to BART station (don't worry about mileage rates just yet) – line 9 car expenses

-   $7 BART fare to SF – (line 9, local transportation)

-   $10 overdue library fines (I'm a bad girl, I know) – line 48 other expenses/research

I used to wait till the end of the year (or late March) before I figured out how many trips on BART I took or how many miles I drove. Big huge hassle.

If it is the only thing you take away from this book, at least purchase a calendar, or set up your spreadsheet. Using it is up to you.

Speaking of mileage, now's a good time to check your odometer reading. Write it in the calendar. Try to estimate what it was on January 1. You'll be needing that information when you calculate mileage for business and pro-rating other car-related expenses on Schedule C. Get in the habit of writing down the starting mileage every January 1.

I suggest adding up business mileage every month from your daily/weekly expense logs and putting the total in the box for the last day of the month and/or the spreadsheet for the month.

N.S. Smith & EM Lynley

Chapter 4: Tackling the Schedule C

If you've taken your first look at the Schedule C, used to report profit or loss from a business, you may find it a bit daunting. It's not as bad as it looks, and it has plenty of useful places to take deductions. I'll go over the key areas which apply to writers, and how to get all the deductions you deserve, while warning you away from the areas that could cause problems.

Let's take a look at the Schedule C form itself. If you use tax prep software, it will probably ask you these questions in approximately this order.

To follow along on a real form, you can download a PDF from the IRS.gov website:

http://www.irs.gov/pub/irs-pdf/f1040sc.pdf

Box A through J

The top part is for your real name and social security number (SSN), which is pretty self-explanatory.

In **box A** put your main business (Writing, Publishing). If you also edit, you can lump this under writing, since it's not your main source of revenue. (See below, Box B for further discussion).

Box B asks for a business code. I'll save you time here so you don't need to search through the instructions.

711510 Independent artists, writers, & performers

511000 Publishing industries (except Internet)

There is no code for "editing" so you can put it under independent writer or under publishing; depending on how it most relates to the way you earn money as an editor. I would suggest putting it under "writing" if you edit under your pen name.

If you edit under the auspices of a publishing company, then put the income/expense under the publishing company. However, to avoid the appearance that your publishing company charges writers to be edited, you may want to keep it under the writing category.

If you run a formatting business, I suggest using "511000 Publishing industries" and keep it separate from your writing business, because it's actually quite different from writing or editing in terms of inputs, outputs, and expenses. That means if you earn money writing *and* formatting, I recommend filing two separate Schedule Cs.

Box C Enter your pen name for "Business name." If you run a publishing company put the company name here.

If you have two or more pen names, use the one which is your primary pen name, or which earns the most money. It's not a big deal to the IRS what you put here. You can also even leave it blank if you like.

Sole proprietorship means you and only you own the company and are responsible for paying all the taxes the company owes. If someone else owns half of it, then you're a partnership and need to file a different form, even if the other owner is a spouse. Each owner is responsible for his share of taxes in a partnership, pro-rated by ownership percentage.

This book is designed to cover only a Schedule C sole proprietorship. There is a special circumstance for married couples who jointly own a business, which is that one spouse can work at the company and receive compensation, rather than a share of profits/loss. You can also elect to be considered a joint venture, where each would file separate Schedule Cs for your share of the business, along with additional forms.

If you both own and operate the business equally in terms of decision-making, you really should set up a legal partnership. Legally, this protects both of you in the event of divorce or separation that might adversely affect the business and future income.

Box D is used only if you obtained an employer ID number (EIN) from the IRS. It is not required, but if you send out 1099-MISC's for anyone who did work for you, or you pay royalties to another author, editor, formatter, or cover artist you should get one. Otherwise, you'll need to put your SSN on the 1099-MISC, which is an invitation to identity theft.

If you pay invoices from independent contractors, you're fine. They don't need your EIN or SSN to report income not on a 1099 (subject to the rules for Line I, which require a 1099-MISC for any individual you pay more than $600 during a calendar year).

Box F: Accounting method: Most individuals use the cash method, which is where you record the expense or revenue on the day you get the check, or the day you spend the money, regardless of when you did the work.

The accrual method is used for manufacturing or certain industries where the expenses and income may be years apart, and it's a way for the IRS to track the relationship between the two much better. Writers often get paid on a quarter or two in arrears, but it's still standard to use the cash method.

Box G: Material participation: did you actively work at the business in terms of time and resources?

This is to distinguish from an investor, rather than a participant.

Box H: self-explanatory

Box I: You are required to file a 1099-MISC with the IRS for anyone to whom you paid more than $600 (or $10 in royalties) during the tax year. You will file a copy with the IRS and give the individual a copy. Some publishers get out of this requirement by calling the royalties "non-employee compensation" which is not necessarily illegal, just inaccurate.

Box J: If you answered Yes to Box I and filed the forms, check "Yes."

Part I: Income

Lines 1-7 cover your gross income, which means how much money you got for the items you sold, subtracting out only the cost of manufacturing or obtaining those items, before you consider any expenses.

If you sold only e-books or sold only through a publisher, your goods won't have any costs.

Income is defined as all money you received from January 1 through December 31.

If you got a check on December 31 and deposit it on Jan 1, it is now income in the new year, since we are using the cash method. It doesn't matter what quarter the royalties are paid on, it matters when the money goes into your bank account. That's the difference between "cash" and "accrual" methods. You must choose one and stick with it forever, or you have to file extra forms for change in accounting technique. Stick with "cash method."

Some publishers won't send you any money until you hit $75 or $100 in accrued royalties. In that case, the income gets counted the quarter you see the money, not the quarter the books were sold. Many distributors don't pay your until the following quarter, and then you'll get paid one quarter later.

Example:

Books sold during 2nd quarter from Amazon.com: Publisher is paid after the end of the second quarter.

Your royalty statement from the publisher will list these sales as 3rd quarter sales (when the publisher got paid and you'll be paid with the third quarter royalties, not the second quarter royalties.

If your publishers pay monthly, then it's hard to tell precisely when you will get paid, but most will pay you as soon as they receive the money from the distributor, so it may only take two months to get Amazon payments rather than three.

Self-publishers, you won't have this problem of being paid that far in arrears, since you'll get the royalties directly from the distributors. The month you get paid is the month you report the income.

Check your contract for information about when you'll be paid for books sold and whether there is a minimum sales threshold before you get the money. If you're paid by check it's more likely there is such a minimum than if you're paid by PayPal. But every publisher and distributor is different, and in some cases you can ask for specific payment method in your contract.

The basic point is that it doesn't matter when the books were sold, only when you received the money. The money you got in January 2013 for books sold during 2012 gets reported on your 2013 tax return. Money you get in January 2014 for books sold during 2013 gets reported as 2014 income (cash method).

As of late 2013, the IRS is in the process of changing requirements with merchants in how income is reported, specifically due to PayPal and credit card companies' ability to make payments to individuals. For 2013 tax returns, however, you will report all income received on line 1.

That includes money received from PayPal/Merchants and on 1099-MISCs from your publishers or distributors. Don't worry about lumping it together, that's the only way to do it now. Your tax software may ask you to list each 1099-MISC separately, in which case do so. That will aid the IRS in matching your reported income with what the publisher reported when they sent in copies of those 1099-MISCs to the IRS.

Line 1 should include:

Amounts received directly from a distributor for self-pubbed titles sold on Amazon, ARe, Kobo, Smashwords, etc., add it all here, regardless of which tax form it was reported on.

Sales of physical books, CDs, or other items at a convention, including any state or local sales tax you collected from the buyers

Sales of items directly from your website, whether downloads or physical.

Sales tax collected on your website or from in-person sales. (We'll expense it out later).

In the future the IRS may go back to separating out income reported on 1099s vs. received from merchants and third parties.

Line 2

Returns and allowances. This covers any money you refunded to customers for sales included in Line 1 or money earned in previous years.

Example 1:

In December 2012 you sold a print book off your website. You counted the revenue in 2012 income.

In January 2013 the customer informed you the package was damaged and wanted their money back, and you refunded the purchase. Include the amount refunded on Line 2. You don't owe tax on the income if the transaction is reversed.

Example 2:

Same December 2012 purchase by customer.

In January 2013, instead of refunding the money, you mail another copy of the book.

This time, you do not count the transaction as a return.

You will remove the copy from inventory, which affects your ending inventory and cost of goods sold.

We're getting a little ahead of ourselves, but don't worry, you won't be including any new income on that transaction, and will get to count the cost of the second copy of the book when accounting for ending inventory.

Line 4 is for Cost of Goods Sold (physical books/discs)

This is used to account for expenses when you hold an inventory of physical books or any other item you manufacture or purchase in order to resell. These items have a cost: purchase or manufacture, unlike e-books which have no cost to produce each individual unit.

I'll skip ahead to Lines 5-7, and cover Cost of Goods Sold in its own section right after.

Lines 5 through 7 are self-explanatory.

This is how much profit you earned for the year before we start subtracting out expenses.

We'll cover Part II: Expenses, in the next chapter.

Part III: Cost of Goods Sold

This section will be easier to follow if you have your copy of the Schedule C while you read it, so you can refer to line numbers and descriptions on the form itself.

If anyone here ever studied Accounting, "cost of goods sold" or COGS is a phrase that will probably bring up not-so-fond memories (FIFO, LIFO, anyone?)

If you never studied Accounting, you're probably even more confused, and with good reason. It's one of the most complicated-looking parts of the Schedule C, though it's not actually that difficult to fill in.

It's the idea of calculating something rather than just adding expenses that terrifies some writers. Doesn't IRS know we're not math whizzes? Otherwise we'd probably be raking in the bucks as programmers!

It looks complicated, but we will take it step by step and you'll get the gist.

First off, why does this even matter?

Great question! It matters because you can deduct the cost of anything you sold against the income you received for it. The IRS puts income and expenses on different lines, which is why the form is more complicated than the concepts in your head.

If you sold print copies at a convention and ended up with $245 in cash, credit cards and Stripe charges, how much of that expense can you write off? The IRS doesn't just let you add up all the purchases when you make them, and then count the income later when you sell them. That would be too easy.

Nope, for IRS purposes and accounting theory businesses are supposed to report inventory costs only when they actually sell the goods. Even though you are not a factory spewing out zillions of widgets or earrings or mouse pads, writers have to follow the same accounting rule.

You will remember that

Line 4 is for Cost of Goods Sold (physical books/discs)
This is used if you hold an inventory of physical books or any other item you manufacture or purchase in <u>order to resell</u>.

If you don't intend to sell it, you don't have to count it. So if you have T-shirts and pens and freebie swag stuff, it doesn't get included here at all.

Cost of Goods Sold is calculated in Part III of the Schedule C.

I'll cover everything here, so you can get the correct figure to put on **Line 4**.

Line 33 Inventory Method

Cost or Lower of Cost or Market

Don't let this confuse you. Just choose COST. It means you value the inventory on the amount it cost you, not the market value. Even if the "market value" is higher, you can only count your actual cost.

Just trust me on this one, but if anyone really wants to know more, you probably should take an accounting class.

The basic method to calculate cost of goods sold is as follows:

Beginning inventory in dollars (January 1 2013 for your 2013 tax return)

+ purchases during the year (in dollars)

- items used for personal purposes (dollar cost of items given to friends, family, etc.).

- ending inventory (Dollar cost of inventory on December 31, 2013)

NOTE: You do not want to subtract out the cost of items used for promotional purposes (giveaways, donations to libraries, or other free items for *business-related* purposes that you could have sold).

You *do* want to make a note of how many copies you gave away in order to track whether it's a useful marketing technique, but these will automatically be removed from ending inventory, so the cost will end up being an indirect deduction.

Your deduction in this case is limited to the cost of the item, not the amount you could have gotten if you sold it.

After you've added all the purchases and subtracted out the personal items and ending inventory, the magical result is the cost of goods sold.

We are just looking at the dollar amounts, not how many, though you will probably need to know both to do this correctly.

What about costs of shipping/postage on your purchases?

For ease calculation, I used whole numbers, but in reality if you purchase books from CreateSpace or your own publisher, chances are you'll be dealing with postage charges and less round numbers.

Include the postage or shipping charges in "purchases" for the Line 36 amount.

Example:

CreateSpace book: 10 copies @ $9.62 = $96.20

Postage: $4.75

Total purchases = $100.95

Example

Walter Writer self-published a book in 2013 about collecting flyswatters.

--He ordered 20 paperback copies from CreateSpace at $10 each February 3, 2013 (purchases of $200)

--He sold 5 books for a total of $25 at a book fair in June

--He did a giveaway on Goodreads of one copy of the paperback in July (we don't count the dollar amount now, but subtract one unit from inventory)

--On December 31 he had 14 copies sitting in the trunk of his car (ending inventory 14 x $10 = $140).

Starting inventory on Jan 1 = 0

Purchases during the year = $200

Ending inventory 14 copies x $10 cost = $140

Walter's cost of goods sold was

$0 + $200 -$140 = $60

If Walter gave a copy to his boss, that would count as a personal use item. You would subtract the $10 cost of the book when calculating Line 36, as well as remove the item from ending inventory, which is now 13 books and $130.

His cost of goods sold would then be

0 + $200 - $10 - $130 = $60

Look! It's the same. That personal-use book is completely ignored in your business expenses. He still only made $25 from selling print copies, for the same $60 cost of the units he actually sold or intended to sell.

The $25 Walter got at the book fair goes into Line 1 (gross receipts and sales). Since his cost of goods sold was $60, and he only got $25, that loss gets incorporated in gross profits and income (line 5 and 7).

Notice the $10 copy he used for the giveaway does not actually get reported anywhere. That loss (or technically, the income he did not receive on that copy) is already factored into the equation. He is never taxed on that, but he does write off the cost when he takes it out of inventory.

If that doesn't make sense, read the last paragraph again. In short, he doesn't earn income, but he can deduct the amount he spent on the book through the reduction in inventory. It's an indirect deduction, rather than a direct deduction (like the cost of printing business cards or airfare to a writers' conference).

So, to sum up how to handle purchases of physical books to sell at an event or to local bookstores:

Do not count the purchase of print copies to resell in any of your expenses in Part II of Schedule C. Save the receipts of all physical copies purchased and calculate your Cost of Goods sold in Part III of the Schedule C.

What if you sell a physical product other than print copies?

I loaded up CDs with copies of my e-books to sell at a convention. How does that fit into the COGS vs. Expenses picture?

You have two options. Choose one or the other, but do not do both.

The easier one:

Add up the cost of the blank CDs, the cases, fancy labels, ribbons or anything else used to produce the end product as "Supplies" on Line 22. Report the expense in the year you buy the items, even if you still have some left over in December.

Make sure to include the money you received on sales in Line 1, Gross receipts and sales.

If you want to use the Cost of Goods Sold method, you can do that instead, though it will be more complicated.

If you make CDs or DVDs with your books to sell, instead of figuring out the cost per book on Line 36, you'll use Line 38 (Materials and supplies) for the cost of the discs, the cases, fancy labels, ribbons or anything else used to produce the end product.

Example:

You spent $50 for CDs and misc. labels during 2013.

You don't have to count up the cost of each CD or the "inventory" of your finished ready-to-sell CDs at the beginning and end of the year.

If you don't also have physical print books, just put your $50 on Line 38.

Make sure to put 0 for both starting and ending inventory (Lines 35 and 41).

Your total Cost of Goods Sold will now be $50.

If you have books too, it will look like this:

Walter from the previous example also made CD copies of his ebooks so he could sell them at the swap meet.

Line 35 Starting inventory =   0

36. Purchases (books) $200

37. Labor $0

38. Supplies (cds, ribbons) $50

39. Other Costs $0

40. Total $250

41. Ending inventory (books) $140

42. COGS $110

Recall, Walter made $25 from selling print books, plus another $10 for selling the CDs.

His gross receipts are $35 for the physical items he sold.

Ending Inventory

If your print copies have different costs, make sure to keep track of how much each one cost so you can accurately value ending inventory.

- You can write the cost in the back of each one in pencil, so at the end of the year you can easily add them up.

- You can keep an inventory spreadsheet which includes the cost of the item, and update it every month or quarter to what you have left, which will give you an inventory snapshot in terms of cost.

Depending on your contract with a publisher, you may be required to remit royalties to them on copies you physically sold. If so, report royalties remitted to your publisher for products you sold yourself on Line 39 (other costs) in the Cost of Goods Sold calculations. It gets subtracted out from earnings automatically.

Sales tax collected on physical sales is included in Gross Receipts and Sales.

Sales tax paid to the state/locality will then be expensed in Part II of Schedule C, not addressed in calculation of Cost of Goods Sold.

Hopefully I've been able to make this a less-confusing section on the Schedule C.

Assignment #2

By now you should already have your calendar. If not, I hope you'll work on keeping track of each assignment.

Part 1

This part of the assignment involves tracking your income, or as the Schedule C calls it "gross receipts."

If you had anything published in 2013, chances are excellent that you recently received some royalties earned during 2013 Q3 and Q4.

Remember, that if you get paid in 2013, it counts as income in 2013. If you've already received some money since January 1, record it as 2014 receipts.

So let's round up your royalty payments and put them into the calendar. I like to use a green highlighter on them, to show income!

I got payments from four different publishers during January, plus an advance, so I'll make entries on the days I deposited the money. Some were made by PayPal and others by paper check. I use the date it was deposited into my account as the date the income was received. That's how the "cash system" of accounting works. Write it down on the day you get the income, or the day you spend it for recording expenses.

Part 2

The next chapter will cover the typical expenses writers incur. Once you're done entering all the income you've received so far this year, collect up all your expense receipts. We'll be talking about what is and is not allowed as expense. If you want to get a head start on entering them, feel free. At least get a feel for what types of items you spent money on.

N.S. Smith & EM Lynley

Chapter 5: Schedule C Part II: Expenses

What Expenses Are Deductible?

This is the million-dollar question and very likely one of the main reasons you bought this book! Don't worry, I'll cover not only typical writer expenses but some not-so-typical expenditures. The IRS breaks expenses up into several categories, and I'll cover each one:

--Start-Up Expenses

--Operating Expenses

--Capital Expenses

--Inventory

Not all categories will apply to each writer, but they are treated differently for tax purposes, so it's important to differentiate the expenses and report them in the correct section of your tax return.

Start-Up Expenses

If you've been running your writing business for more than one full tax year, this section won't apply to you. For 2013 tax returns, you must have started your writing business during calendar year 2013 to claim start-up expenses. If you started earlier but didn't classify expenses as "start-up expenses," you can choose to file an amended return for the applicable tax year, but only do so if there is a significant change in your refund after. Amendments for small changes are more likely to flag future returns for closer scrutiny.

If you started your business during the past tax year, you may choose to categorize some of your expenses as start-up expenses. It's up to you, but it may not give you the best tax refund. However, the IRS won't expect a profit during your start-up year, so it may be the best time to buy some equipment that normally gets depreciated, like a new computer, desk, etc., and write it all off at once.

If you're still unpublished and haven't yet filed taxes for your writing expenses, you may find it makes more sense to write off allowable start-up costs now,

If 2014 is the year you start your writing business, this may be the time to buy a computer, some office supplies, other office equipment, membership in the relevant writing association(s) for your genre, etc., and take a loss—assuming you can afford the expenditures.

Later, once you start earning more writing income, you'll want to adjust expenses to make sure you don't keep incurring losses. That's where the Hobby Loss Rule comes in. And it's why you should aim to know your profit/loss situation at least at the end of every quarter. You wouldn't want to buy a computer or make a big expenditure later only to find it gives you three years of losses in a row.

What Qualifies as a Start-up Cost?

The IRS defines start-up costs as those incurred before you start operating your business.

If you run a flower store, it's pretty clear that the day you open the door and hang up the "Grand Opening" sign that you're open. But how do you determine this for a writing business?

Since running a business means having a product and trying to sell it, "open for business" would mean that you have written something and have submitted to a publisher, even if you haven't yet gotten a contract or received any money for it. You may already be running a business even if you haven't earned a penny.

If you haven't written a story yet, but are determined to become a professional writer, then you can claim expenses to prepare you for the task. That would mean a new computer, a desk, some books about writing and even a class about writing or running a business would be considered appropriate start-up costs.

If you've written a story but never sent it to a publisher, then you can technically claim the same type of expenses, since you haven't yet begun operating a writing business: you haven't tried to sell your product.

If you've written stories and got a pile of rejection letters, you'll need to separate out which expenses you incurred as start-up costs and which are operating expenses, based on when you spent the money for each item.

For self-publishers, the "start date" could be the date you published your first book. You could justify to the IRS that until that point, your business was not open, even if you were writing. You could write off books about self-publishing purchased before the "start date" as start-up costs. Anything purchased after that date would be operating expenses, which are next up for discussion.

Whatever date and rationale you use, I suggest you write in your expense calendar/log/spreadsheet what date is your "start date." This will be need for pro-rating partial year expenses, and the IRS will ask you if they ever take a closer look at your returns.

Because the IRS can legally question any prior year return, make sure you keep this start-up/start date information on file permanently. It could be several years down the road before the IRS ever contacts you, and you should be able to provide this information at any time.

Operating Expenses

This is the meat of your deductible expenses as a writer. While you may have a good idea of what's deductible, you may not know which category to report the expenses. Or you may not be sure whether something is deductible. You should find answers to most of your questions here.

The IRS guidelines say "ordinary and necessary." expenses may be deducted from business income. So, what's ordinary and what's necessary? There are no hard and fast rules, because what's allowable differs by industry and for writers, by project.

A horse trainer can write off a whip, and so can a BDSM writer. If you write automotive articles, chances are the IRS won't accept a whip as a business expense, but you can probably write off four sets of windshield wipers, if you were writing an article about them. For now, don't worry about whether you actually sold the article or earned any royalties on the book. Don't even worry about whether you finished writing the book.

Ask yourself: would I buy this item or book if I wasn't writing this book or if I wasn't a writer in this particular genre? (We're back to the whip...)

There is quite a lot of leeway here, but it's not a free-for-all. The most common expenses for writers include: computers, printers, office supplies, books about writing, books in your genre, books used for research, cost of travel for research, promo, education, seminars, conferences, bank charges, cost of editing, cover art and publishing services.

I wrote a novella about BDSM several years ago—well before the whole *Fifty Shades of Grey* phenomenon erupted. Maybe too early. At the time. I didn't know anything about BDSM, so I took a class at a local dungeon. Of course I wrote the cost off. I even put "Flogging Class" down on my Schedule C. I was kind of hoping the IRS would ask me about it. I couldn't wait to see the agent's face when I explained.

I write off the cost of books to do research, classes about writing, promo/swag items and online ads.

Tricky situations occur are when you purchase an item that is used for both writing and personal use. If possible, try to separate them by purchasing separate items if it makes sense. One of the biggest beefs the IRS has is claiming personal expenses as business expenses. Phones and computers fall into this category. I personally don't claim my cell phone purchase price, but I claim a portion of the monthly cell phone bill, based on what percentage of phone use is business-related.

If you already have a computer at home and purchase a new one for your writing, you can write it off as a writing expense (or depreciate it, depending on the cost and type of computer). Keep the old one for predominantly personal use, and it makes it easier to justify claiming the full purchase price of a new computer for your writing business.

If you have two different writing-related businesses--writing and publishing--you'll need to pro-rate your expenses, rather than write everything off of both returns. You can't claim the full price of same computer for both your writing business and your publishing business. It's precisely this double-dipping is that gets people in trouble. If you spend about 30% of your time on writing and 70% on publishing, use that ratio. If some items have different ratios, apply the correct one, and then document it somewhere about how you made that determination.

Not sure about the ratios? Go back to the brand new calendar. For one month, write down every day how many hours you spent on each enterprise.

March 1: Writing 2 hours. Publishing 0

March 2: Writing 1 hour. Publishing 2 hrs.

At the end of the month, calculate the ratio. If it varies wildly from month to month, keep track for 3 months, then use the average. If you document, you have a rationale the IRS can feel comfortable with, even if it's not completely accurate. Undocumented guessing invites further intrusion and audits.

In my tax practice I have plenty of Schedule C clients who don't keep track of expenses very well, if at all. For these people, the numbers are written on the ceiling. "How much did you spend on advertising?" Client looks at the ceiling and sighs a few times, then says "$500." "How much on supplies?" Glance to the ceiling. "$500."

Uh-uh.

Keep track of your spending, even if you don't have a receipt. That calendar I suggested earlier will come in handy here. The IRS does accept such "expense logs" even if you can't come up with a receipt.

I'll get into more detail on what writers can and cannot deduct when we go line by line through the expense section of Schedule C.

Capital Expenses

These are assets that have a useful life of more than one year: computers, furniture, reference books, land, buildings, vehicles. As you can see, not much applies for writers.

Generally these assets are depreciated, which means you write off a portion of the purchase price each year until you've written off the full amount. For computers, you can write the full price off in the first year using the special 179 expense option, rather than over five or seven years. I suggest calling small items "supplies" or writing off as other expenses rather than going through the trouble of depreciating something that didn't cost much. If your computer or desk is going to send you into the red for the year you buy it, and you're flirting with too many losses with the hobby-loss rule, then you might consider depreciating the more expensive items. But the IRS is really looking at preventing companies from writing off the full price items that cost tens of thousands of dollar or much more, for larger-scale businesses that use machinery and factories. Your new PC isn't going to rock their boat.

Inventory

Do you have a stack of print books you sell directly to readers at conventions or book signings? Do you sell direct to bookstores? If you make up CDs, DVDs or flash drives full of your writing that you sell, you will need to account for inventory when you file your return.

You are not taxed on the level of inventory you hold, so if you have stacks and stacks of books sitting in your office (or trunk of your car) it does not affect your bottom line.

If you recall from the section on Cost of Goods Sold, you won't get to claim the cost of the books until you sell them or remove them from inventory in some way.

Chapter 6: Deducting Expenses on Schedule C

Lines 8-17

Line 8 is for items or services you purchased for promotion of yourself or your books.

I'm a huge fan of Line 8 Advertising. I call my website, domain name, swag pens and business cards, online ads, Facebook ads, LiveJournal account fees, etc., as "advertising."

Did you do a giveaway? Put down the cost of prizes you purchased on Line 8, such as gift certificates, e-readers, T-shirts, etc.

Do not include the cost of items taken out of inventory (e.g., paperbacks). We'll cover those in the discussion of inventories and Cost of Goods Sold (COGS) in a later chapter.

Do you have a promotional company working for you? Did you pay for someone to design your website or make banner ads? If you purchased stock photos for the web designer or artist to use, add them in here. This is the place to deduct those expenses.

Line 9

Car and Truck Expenses

If you drive your own car for business-related purposes you have two choices: taking a deduction based on mileage, or using a percentage of actual expenses (gas, insurance, deductible portion of license plates, interest on car loan, repairs, etc.,), pro-rated for the business use. Once you choose a method, you must stick with it for that particular vehicle.

I strongly suggest using mileage. In most cases your ratio of business to other use is small, so you won't get as large a deduction for actual expenses, and that method requires you to keep both more paperwork and justify the ratio you've used.

The business mileage rate from January 1- December 31, 2013 is 56.5 cents per mile. As of publication, the 2014 rate will be 56 cents per mile

You can include mileage between your home (or other office location) and bookstores, libraries, location of any classes, business-related meetings, even trips to the airport when you fly to a conference.

Add up all those trips to RWA or MWA meetings. Did you meet a writing buddy for coffee and crit? Did you go to meet another author at a signing? I went to another author's book launch party, several book signings and a few lectures. I drove my editor to the airport when she came to visit. I drove down to Monterey and Big Sur to research a location with another writer. I drove to spend Christmas with another writer and spent a significant portion of time talking about writing and the business of writing. I attend monthly meetings of a writers' organization. All those miles add up to a nice deduction.

Caveat on mileage (a true story). Another tax preparer I work with had a real estate agent client. We all know how many miles Realtors drive for business— plenty. This client did not make notes of how many miles he drove with clients and only gave an estimate when he filed his return. He got audited. Since he didn't have *any mileage log* the IRS disallowed the *entire* mileage deduction, even though everyone (including the IRS auditor) agreed he drove for work. The IRS doesn't have gray. It's black or white: no receipt or log, no deductions, even one that's a reasonable estimate.

So, even if you don't have a receipt, write it on the calendar. You can bring the whole calendar in for your audit and the IRS will probably believe everything you wrote in there as long as it's reasonable.

If you've been keeping track of total miles driven for the year, you can calculate the percentage of miles driven for your writing business. You will use this ratio for other deductions later on.

Example:

2000 miles driven for writing businesses out of 12,000 miles total driven for calendar 2012 = 16.7% use of vehicle for business.

Did you have local public transportation expenses? Those actually get counted under Car and Truck Expenses.

If you have local tolls and parking, add that to the mileage amount because it is part of what you spent to use your car for business.

Did you use the local bus, subway, local train, etc. for business-related trips? That gets reported on Line 9 all. My use of BART in San Francisco goes here because it's not an overnight trip, even though technically it's not a car expense, it's all lumped together basically as "non-overnight transportation expenses."

Transportation expenses incurred on an overnight trip are reported on Line 24a Travel

Expenses. Keep track of them as well, but don't add them into Line 9.

Line 10 Commissions and fees

This is unlikely to apply to most writers. Publishers may want to put royalties paid to their authors on this line. However, if you paid commissions or fees to a distributor (on top of them taking their cut of the royalties), then report the amount here.

If you published a book under your name or business name for another author and you received royalties from a distributor which you later paid to the other author, put them here. This way you do not pay tax on them, even though they are included on a 1099-MISC you got from the distributor.

Example:

Jonathan is a computer programmer who wrote a book during 2013. His wife Dorothy is a full-time writer and she published his book on Amazon/KDP on her account.

During 2013 Amazon paid Dorothy $1560 total, including $60 of royalties for Jonathan's books.

Dorothy counts all $1560 in her earnings, then she puts $60 paid to Jonathan on Line 10. Now the $60 does not get taxed as Dorothy's earnings.

She can give Jonathan a 1099-MISC if she wants to completely document the transaction. If this amount was over $600 she would be required to use the 1099-MISC to report the transfer of funds.

Jonathan can report the $60 as hobby income on Line 21 of his 1040 form. If he had expenses, he can deduct up to $60 as hobby expenses on Schedule A, or he can decide to file his own Schedule C if he wants to establish a separate writing business for himself.

Line 11 Contract labor

Include amounts paid to cover artists, editors, or anyone you paid to help you produce your product, which in most cases is a book or story. If you paid someone to produce an ebook (file conversion), include it here. If you paid by check, note the check number. If the person invoiced you for the services, keep the invoice.

However, if you paid separately for stock photos to be used on *covers*, I suggest putting that amount under other expenses.

Important reminder here: If you pay any one *person* more than $600 for services related to producing your work, you are required to issue them a 1099-MISC and file a copy with IRS. You will need their SSN, and to avoid identity theft, get yourself an EIN (employer identification number) if you must issue these documents, otherwise you will have to put your own SSN on the form.

You do not need to file a 1099-MISC if you pay a *company* for services, only an individual or another sole proprietor.

Ask each of your subcontractors (editor, artist, and formatter) to fill in form W-9 as early in the year as possible, so you know what your responsibilities are for paperwork and withholding.

If the contract labor provider is in another country, make sure they fill in form W-8BEN and keep this on file. It prevents you from getting in trouble for not withholding tax on payments for anyone who did not provide you with a W-9 form.

Line 13 Depreciation

If you purchase items such as furniture, some computer equipment or anything which lasts more than one year, you generally cannot write off the full expense in the year you purchase it. Instead, you write off a portion of the cost over the life of the item. Electronics and computer equipment get special treatment.

Through 2013 there is special treatment under Section 179 that allows most businesses to write off the full amount of certain items (all the items a writer would use are covered, so don't sweat the details on this one) in the year purchased. Because of that provision, you can generally ignore the depreciation section and write off the full amount of a computer, electronic equipment and the like as "other expenses."

Example:

In Section V of Schedule C:

HP Computer: $600

WD External Drive: $125

Misc. cables/mouse/etc.: $37

Total these amounts and put on Line 48.

If you start using a personal item for business, you can only depreciate the remaining value. It's pretty complicated, and I recommend having an accountant handle this for you, or be sure to use the business version of tax software, which will guide you through the series of questions to determine how much you can depreciate.

For most people who do not rely on writing as their sole source of income, the amount of depreciation is going to be negligible. If your writing income is low and you buy yourself a fancy desk and start listing depreciation on your Schedule C, it's going to grab attention. It's another reason why you want to carefully consider which purchases to make and to deduct, based on the amount of income you are actually generating.

Lines 14 and 15 won't apply to the majority of writers.

Line 16 Interest

16Aa: This is for mortgage interest paid on a building wholly owned by your business (not for business use of home, to be discussed later).

16B: "Other interest" would include interest paid on a business loan or business charges on a credit card. This is one reason to keep business charges on a separate card if you possibly can, to make it easier to calculate your deduction. If you mix them, you can calculate the approximate amount of interest paid on business charges by using the percentage of total amount charged as a guideline.

Example:

--You charged $10,000 during the year on your credit card, a mix of business and personal.

--$2,000 was for business-related expenses.

--Business use of card is 20%

--Total interest paid on card during 2012 was $1000

Business-related interest deduction is $200 (20% of total interest paid on the card).

For the sake of completeness, include a note in your tax records folder on how you calculated this figure. You won't need to include it with your tax return, but if three years from now the IRS asks how you came up with $200 here, you'll have a reasonable explanation for the process you used.

Remember, the IRS likes to know how you calculated anything that doesn't have a receipt, so the more documentation the better. It takes a minute or two now, and much longer later on to recall. Plus, the longer you wait to include notes to justify your numbers or process, the less likely the IRS will buy your explanation in the event they request more information or an audit, even if it's perfectly reasonable. Err on the side of over explaining.

Line 17 Legal and Professional Service
This is for legal or accounting services, including bookkeeping and tax preparation.

How much did it cost to have your taxes done? Put it down. If your Schedule C caused you to need the services of an accountant, rather than doing it yourself, only count the additional expense over what you would pay to do your personal taxes.

You can deduct fees paid to an accountant or tax preparer or for the cost of software and the filing fees if not included.

Example:

Your accountant charged you $500 to do your taxes, including Schedule C. He would only charge $200 for your personal tax return, so you can deduct the extra amount ($300) on the Schedule C. The cost of personal tax preparation can be deducted on Schedule A.

Lines 18-27b

Line 18 Office Expense

This is for little expenses you incur in running your office, not in producing your "product." It's most often used for postage, envelopes, copying, faxing charges, or little things like that in the case of writers.

Line 19 Pension and Profit Sharing – not relevant to this discussion

Line 20 Rent or leasing costs of equipment to product your product or other business property.

This mainly applies to manufacturing or businesses which need special equipment. However, if you rent or lease furniture or computer equipment, this is the place to include those expenses. Rental cars used for business travel get included under Line 24.

Line 21 Repairs and Maintenance – expenses for maintaining the building. If you use part of your home for business, see below. This really only applies if the business owns the building.

Line 22 Supplies

This is intended for materials used in the business that get used up during the year. Pens, notebooks, index cards, and the like. These are items that don't normally get inventoried or counted or even noticed. It's more applicable to say a doctor's office that uses cotton balls or syringes and doesn't necessary keep track of every single piece used. It's a good catch-all for little things you don't quite know where else to put, but it's for physical items.

I do use it for notebooks, stamps, postage spent on items mailed for business, tape, envelopes, folders, desk accessories. You can also use it for small electronic supplies and accessories like a cell phone case and stylus for your tablet.

If the item in question is used partly for business and partly for personal, deduct only a pro-rated amount on your Schedule C.

If the item is used in two businesses on two separate Schedules C, pro-rate the amount between the two based on the percentage use for each.

Example:

You bought an iPad which you use for business and personal use. The cover and other accessories came to $150. You use it one-third of the time for business.

Deduct $50 in supplies for the iPad accessories ($150 x 1/3).

You cannot deduct the personal use amount.

Line 23 Taxes and licenses

Include any sales tax you paid on physical books or other items **you sold to others**.

That means if you have a booth at a convention and you are required to collect sales tax and remit to state or local government. If you sell books (electronic or physical) off your own website you may need to collect sales tax for customers in your own state and send the amount to the state. Each state has different rules, so check your state's laws now if you don't know them.

Add up any sales tax you collected and sent on. (The amount of tax collected should have been included in your income since you are going to deduct out the amount you don't keep)

Example:

You sold 100 paperbacks at $10 each and are required to collect and remit 8% sales tax to your state.

You collected $1080 from customers.

Include $1080 in Line 1 "gross receipts" since you received the full amount.

Deduct $80 on Line 23 as sales tax paid to your state.

Result: you are only taxed on the $1000 that account for the sales of the books.

If you have to pay a business license in your state, county or city, include the fee here. You may need a special permit to sell at a convention; deduct that cost here. Requirements may differ state to state, so check your own particular state and city to see if you need any licenses or whether you must pay sales tax on items you sell direct to customers.

Line 24a and b Travel Expenses

This is a big expense—and a big question mark—for many of us. In my case, it's the largest expense on the entire Schedule C.

These expenses are generally for overnight trips.

Here I add up all my airfares, hotels, and other transportation incurred on trips related to the business of writing.

- conventions

- visits to the office your editor or publisher

- trips to your co-author's house for writing or research

- trips primarily for research purposes

- writing courses held in other locations

If you have a writing partner who lives in another state, you can write off a trip to visit him if the purpose of the trip is to work on your joint project. If you spend half the trip just socializing, then deduct only half of the expenses.

Line 24a Travel Expenses

For any trip which is primarily for your business, you can take a deduction for the full cost of transportation and travel, including taxis, tips to the bellboy, car rental or the airport shuttle. You can get back that $20 American Airlines charged you to check your bag. Did the hotel charge you $30 a day to park your car? Deduct it. Wi-Fi fees in the room? Deduct it.

The best part about hotel bills is they itemize everything, so you know exactly how much you spent and for what items. Keep a copy of the bill in the folder with your other receipts. Cross out any personal expenses or mark them "Personal" and the IRS will think you're extra careful not to mix business with personal expenses.

If you rent a car on a business trip, you will deduct the cost of gas as a travel expense, rather than recording the mileage. The mileage deduction discussed earlier is for business use of your *personal* vehicle.

However: if you take a personal side trip while on business, you cannot deduct the cost of gasoline, tolls, parking, etc., for that particular trip.

> **Example:** You go to a writers' conference in New Orleans. You arrive a day early and rent a car to drive to a plantation for sightseeing. This is not part of the business aspect of the trip, so you can't include the cost of the car, gas, food or any other expense of the sightseeing, UNLESS you use (and document) this trip as research for a story.

Document everything you include on Lines 24a and b, and carefully consider whether it was a business expense or not.

High travel deductions compared to low earnings are a red flag for the IRS. While they may not necessarily disallow a deduction, this is something likely to be scrutinized if they start asking questions about whether you are a business or a hobby.

If your earnings are low, be conservative in your deductions here and take extra efforts to document how the trip was *necessary* to your *business* (as opposed to necessary for your writing in general). Remember that the adjective "necessary" is part of the requirement to deduct it. If your trip to RT wasn't necessary to running your business, don't deduct it as a business expense.

If you take a lot of research trips but don't write or sell much, the IRS will notice. Be conservative. You can always amend a prior year return if you end up writing and selling a book about New Orleans, so you can still deduct the research expenses later.

If you are consistently profitable, then make sure you count every penny, but still do not forget to document it.

Line 24b Meals and Entertainment

KEY INFORMTION HERE: you can deduct only half of your meals and entertainment, even when it's for business. IRS figures you have to eat anyway, so the expense isn't solely because of your writing business.

If you set a book in Thailand and go to a Thai restaurant for research (both of which I did), you can still only expense half of it. However, if you take a class on Thai cooking in order to do research, then put it under "other expenses" and not under meals or entertainment.

Lunch with your co-author: 50% write off.

Lunch with your publisher: make sure they paid, and not you! But they can still only write off half of that lunch.

What about using the per diem for meals while on business travel?

A lot of business travelers use per diem rates set by the government rather than fiddling with receipts for lunches, dinners and random trips to Starbucks. That's fine when you're an employee. When you're self-employed, you can only write off 50% of such expenses, which means half of that per-diem amount, not the full amount. You'll probably come out ahead using the receipts for your actual expenses.

Line 25 Utilities

I use this line to report internet service and cell phone. Since I use mine for personal use as well, I pro-rate them for the amount used for my business. If you use your home for business, do not put house utilities charges here. Those will go on a separate form when you calculate business use of home.

However, if you use your home landline for business, you cannot deduct it. You can only deduct any secondary lines or additional phone charges incurred by the business, above the cost of the "base service."

Line 26 Wages

Wages paid to employees who get W-2 forms only. Recall that wages for 1099-MISC labor is already included earlier on the form.

Most writers don't have employees. However, if you're raking in the bucks and have a personal assistant employee, lucky you. Report their wages here.

Line 27 Other Expenses

Here's where I put in what I spent on conference *registration* fees, sponsorships for events (though that could go under advertising instead. Just don't try to write the same thing off twice).

Dues for a professional writers' organization such as RWA, MWA, Sisters in Crime, SFWA, etc., go here. Whatever your genre or specialty, there is an organization for it.

I write off half my Netflix subscription because I use it watch films/documentaries for research. I add in books I've purchased for research.

Example:

I wrote a book about a Napa Valley winemaker. Several of the books I purchased for research were on the topics of winemaking and issues in Napa Valley as a result of the influx of Silicon Valley money.

It's clear the books were research for that novel.

If you buy books about something you never write about, think carefully how you will explain that deduction if the IRS comes-a-knocking.

I never buy a book that I can find at the local library. I tend to scour the shelves before I even choose a topic or locale for a novel, which is how I keep my expenses fairly low, even though I often use twenty or thirty resources per novel.

Did you buy specialized software for writing (like Scrivener or even a new version of Microsoft Office) or for record keeping, like QuickBooks? Write it off here.

What about books in your own genre?
I call this *market research*. It's standard in every industry to spend some money to find out what the competition is up to and try to learn something from it. Why can't writers do the same thing? It's a bit trickier here because most of us love to read the genre we write. That makes it even more important to differentiate simply writing off all your book purchases with true market research. How? *Document.*

Example

Author XYZ is always at the top of the charts. You want to know what she's doing that you aren't. Buy a few of her books and mark it in your calendar of expenses as "Market research: books by XYZ, (include book titles)."

Then, after you read them, write up a few notes on your conclusions. Not a book review, but a market-research oriented comment to show you didn't just read those books for fun. "Lots of sex scenes, has characters who ....."

Don't abuse this. Writing off $500 of book purchases as market research when you had $200 of revenue is going to get noticed.

I also include as "Other expenses" fees paid for writing courses which are not at a regular university, college or community college. I'll address writing courses and IRS educational credits in more detail later.

Writing courses

As some of you know, the IRS has several education credits available for taxpayers who pay educational expenses. The largest of these is the American Opportunity Credit, but it also includes the Tuition and Fees Deduction and the Lifetime Learning Credit. Unfortunately, to take any of these credits, you must pay tuition at a "qualifying educational institution," which is defined by the IRS as one which is eligible for Department of Education-funded financial aid programs.

So, unless you take a class at a university or community college, you won't qualify for one of the IRS education credits.

But, you can *deduct* work-related education expenses. The rule is that the class must be used to improve or maintain skills needed in your *present* work. Note the use of italics. What it means is you cannot take a class and write it off if you are using it to gain skills for a new line of work.

However, you can deduct course fees for classes done online such as Savvy Authors, the many RWA online courses and the like, if they are about writing or the business of writing. If you are a romance writer and you take a course on mystery writing, it's not a new line of work. It's still writing.

If you are a writer and you take a class about how to run a publishing business, well that one isn't going to be a qualified expense against your writing income. That's a new line of work (Remember those business codes I mentioned earlier, if you take a class about how to become something classified under a different business code, it's a new line of work).

If you take a live class, you can write off your mileage and parking. You can write off the cost of books required for the class. If you have to stay overnight or travel to another location for the main purpose of the trip, you can deduct travel, meals (50%) and lodging, subject to the same rules as other travel business expenses. So, if you go to San Diego for the main purpose of the writers' conference, you can deduct the related travel expenses for the trip. If you go to visit your aunt and decide to pop in for a day at the writers' conference, the IRS probably won't figure it out, but if you spend more time on personal activities than educational activities, you aren't supposed to deduct your lodging and meals for the time you are engaged in personal activities.

Example:

You go to San Diego for the writers' conference, which lasts two days. You stay an extra day to visit Aunt Tilly for a total of three nights in a hotel.

You can write off the airfare or mileage (since the main purpose of the trip was the conference), two nights of lodging and two days of meals. You should not write off the third night's lodging or the meals on the day you are hanging with your aunt.

The IRS has special rules for education conducted on cruises and outside of the United States. If you have such expenses, let me know and I will research the restrictions for you.

Did you include everything you can possibly deduct? One of my tricks before I finish my taxes is to comb my credit card statements, bank statement and PayPal statements. If you keep all your writing-business charges to a separate account, this takes less time. But I do go over everything to make sure I've counted every purchase and classified it by type, according to which line on the Schedule C it applies, advertising, research, transportation, etc.

I print out extra copies of these statements and write down what each expense was for right next to the amount. That's part of my expense log in case I get audited. There are always things I missed writing into my calendar.

Final Calculations

The rest of Schedule C determines your net profit or loss and how much loss may be deducted from other income.

Line 28 – Sum of lines 8 through 27a.

Line 29 Tentative profit (Line 7 – Line 28)

Line 30 Business use of home.
I'll touch on a few points here and then discuss details in a separate chapter, since it's kind of tricky. They made big changes to the laws for 2013, which may affect some of you.

You'll notice that this expense shows up after "tentative profit." There is a reason for that. You cannot deduct business use of home unless you have a *profit* first. The rationale behind this is so small businesses aren't tempted to write off a lot of their home expenses against their main ("day job") income which normally would not be deductible.

You only get this luxury if your business earns a profit. But you can only deduct business use of home up to the amount of profit. Again, this is to keep you from deducting home expenses against regular income.

Example 1:

Walter Writer made a tentative business profit of $2000 last year.

--His business use of home expenses came to $2500.

--He can only write off $2000, which gives him a Net Profit on Schedule C Line 31 of $0.

Example 2:

Wanda Writer, Walter's wife, writes books about mushrooms.

--Her tentative results were a loss of $500 in 2013.

--She had business use of home of $2000 (her office is smaller), but Wanda *cannot* claim any of it on Schedule C.

She takes her $500 loss from Schedule C Line 32 and can deduct it against her "day job" income on Line 12 of the Form 1040.

(NOTE: She will include Walter's Schedule C income or loss and put the sum on Line 12. In our examples he broke even after his allowable business use of home deduction, and she has a loss for a net Line 12 entry of -$500 on their joint return.

Example 3:

Andi Author had a tentative profit of $2000 last year.

Her business use of home was $1000.

Her Net Profit on Schedule C Line 31 is $1000. She will put this on her Form 1040 Line 12.

That's it for the main expense sections of the Schedule C.

Line 31

Net profit or loss

Subtract business use of home from tentative profit.

Line 32

If you have a loss, the IRS wants to know if all your investment is at risk. What this is getting at is whether this is a passive loss or an active loss.

The rules for how much loss you can deduct against other income differ. If you are actively running your writing or self-publishing business, making decisions and stand to be out every dollar you spent if you don't make a profit, mark box A.

Chapter 7: Home Office Deduction

Qualifying Home Office

Whether you own or rent your place, you can take a home office deduction, as long as your office qualifies.

There's good news in 2014 for anyone with a home office. The IRS has created a simplified method to calculate your home office deduction starting in tax year 2013. This benefits both renters and home owners, and will save you a lot of time and calculations—if you have a qualified home office.

Be forewarned, this is an area where the IRS can get very particular. So, let's start with what qualifies as a home office.

A home office is a place where you *regularly* and *exclusively* conduct your business.

For writers, it's often hard to pin down our "business" to a specific location, especially if you do research outside of your "office," write at a café, library or in the park on a sunny day.

Writing or researching away from your office won't prevent you from claiming a home office, as long as you do a lot of your writing and other writing-related work in the designated home-office area.

Do you have your own desk where you sit for a good portion of your writing, promo, online activities and bookkeeping? That's a start to meeting the definition.

The key to "exclusive" doesn't mean you do your work only there, but that you do *only work* and don't do other non-business activities there. If you want to email your mom, that's okay, but it's not okay to groom the dog, sew a quilt, or help your kid do his homework in your office space.

If you wouldn't do it at your office in a big company, don't do it in your home office.

You don't necessarily need an entire room to yourself. If you have a desk in one corner of the living room, and your bookshelves with writing and research resources are nearby, and you write here while other family members are out of the house, then that's sufficient to delineate an office area.

However, if it's a share space and other people are regularly using it for other purposes, it doesn't qualify. It's fine if your kids or spouse use the desk occasionally, but it shouldn't be a dual-purpose area that is used when you are not writing for a variety of other activities.

The larger the proportion of your home the "office" occupies, the more likely the IRS will ask for proof that the space is used regularly and exclusively for your business.

Measure only the space used for your desk and bookshelves. Take a photo of the area in case the IRS asks you to prove you've got this space and that it's not used for anything else.

A desk in a busy common area that isn't conducive to writing or working doesn't qualify because you probably aren't doing most of your writing work at that desk. An office in the guest bedroom would qualify if you rarely have guests who would disrupt your work. However, if the room is frequently in use for other activities, then it's not exclusively your workspace.

Key points:

You do most of your writing, promotion, bookkeeping, etc., in the home-office space (used regularly for your writing business)

You do not do other activities in this space (used exclusively for your business)

Other family members do not use the space on a regular basis.

Measure the space

Remember these expenses are subtracted off your Schedule C *profits*, so unless you make a profit at writing, you cannot deduct any home office expenses. If you made money, the home office is an additional allowable expense, but only to the extent of your profits. You can't incur a Schedule C loss through use of your home, no matter how big or exclusive your office is.

Using the Simplified Method

Let's start with the easy new method.

You can take $5/square foot, up to $1500 per year, pro-rated by the number of days you were in business.

Example 1:

You are an established writer, who was in business for the whole of 2013.

Your office area is half of the extra bedroom (12 x 10 feet), giving you an area of 6 feet by 10 feet for office use.

Your simplified deduction is 60 x $5 = $300

Example 2:

You started writing in 2013 and submitted your first story in October. You didn't actually make a space for your home office until August, but since then you use that 60 square foot space for writing and promo work regularly.

You can't take the full home office deduction since you didn't have an office the full year. You can take the deduction for 5 months (August-December).

60 x $5 x 5/12 = $125 deduction for 2013

If you use the space for all of 2014, you will be able to take the full deduction when you file your 2014 taxes.

(End of example)

You will enter this information on **Schedule C, Line 30.**

But that's not all, folks! There may still be more you can deduct under the simplified rules.

If you own your house, you can now take the full deduction for mortgage interest and real estate taxes on Schedule A (Personal Itemized Deductions). You no longer have to pro-rate these deductions for the personal-use area only.

You no longer get the deduction for depreciation with the simplified method, but you also don't have to hassle with an extra set of forms this entails. Use of the simplified method also eliminates the depreciation recapture requirement when selling the home. You still have to recapture the accumulated depreciation taken in prior years, however.

Since the calculation is on the main Schedule C, it should also make your tax return less expensive, if you use a tax preparation company that has surcharges for additional forms and worksheets. (The depreciation schedules alone rack up a hefty charge).

Calculating the Deduction Old School

If you've taken a home office deduction in the past, you may discover the amount allowed under the simplified method is probably lower than what you are used to, even when allowing for the additional mortgage interest deduction on Schedule A. You can still use the old method if it results in a larger deduction. It's up to you.

The second method for calculating your home office deduction is far more complicated, though for most people it will very likely result in a higher deduction.

The deduction is calculated as a percentage of your total home or apartment costs. If your office space is 100 square feet and your home is 1000 square feet, then you can deduct 10% of the cost of running your home.

You will need to fill in IRS Form 8829 (Business Use of Your Home), which requires you to calculate the area used for business as a percentage of the whole area of your home, then you include cost of a variety of typical expenses for a house: mortgage interest, insurance, utilities, real estate taxes, or rent if you don't own the home.

Form 8829 at IRS.gov

Download a copy of the form and look at it as we go through the explanation.

Part I

Line 1: put down the square footage of your office area as defined above.

Line 2: total square footage of house or apartment. If you don't know it, the figure should be in your purchase documentation, otherwise measure as carefully as you can.

Line 3: calculate the percentage of home used for business purposes.

Line 4-6: ignore these unless you also run a daycare facility.

Line 7: copy line 3

Part II

Record the total amount of rent, insurance, utilities, repairs, etc., done on the entire house and then subtract a pro-rata portion from your business profits as calculated on Line 29 of Schedule C.

Things get a bit more complicated if you own your own house because you'll need to deal with depreciation. If you use tax preparation software, you will be prompted for information about the purchase price of the home, the value of the land, the date you bought it and the date you started using the home office. If you prefer not to deal with these details, you can just ignore it and calculate the deduction based on your other expenses.

Caveat: Even if you do not take the depreciation deduction when using the standard method, you will be expected to account for and recapture the depreciation when you sell this house. The accumulated depreciation is subtracted from basis, which means it is considered profit. You will be taxed on that amount because the IRS assumes you took the deduction. It's complicated, which may steer you in the direction of the simplified method.

There are two columns for home office expenses: direct and indirect.
- Direct is for expenses which pertain only to your business.

- Indirect is something paid for the whole house, which cannot easily be separated as business/non-business, such as a new roof. You can't just put roof over one part or the other.

Rent is another example of an indirect expense. Unless you pay a separate rent for the office space, then include the total rent paid on your house/apartment in "indirect" and it will be pro-rated as part of the calculation of the form.

Homeowners, keep in mind that you cannot deduct your full mortgage payment under the home-office deduction. You may include only the *interest* portion of the payment, not the amount that goes toward principle. The IRS does not give you a deduction for purchasing a personal capital asset.

Utilities may have both a direct and indirect expense: Include the cost of electricity, gas and water for the whole house (indirect) as well as cable TV (if you use it for business) and telephones. If you have a second landline, deduct it here as a direct expense (if exclusively used for your business).

Do not deduct cell phone charges here since they are not part of your house, unless the cell service is part of a bundle and cannot be separated from the telephone or cable charges. In that case, put the bundle charge in the "indirect" column, which allows you deduct a portion of the total cost.

Insurance is another indirect expense: you don't pay a separate charge just for your business space, at least as a writer. If you run a food-related business, you might have specific extra insurance, but that would most likely have gone on the Schedule C, and not here.

Most of the expenses here are self-explanatory.

Remember: if you only used your home office for part of the year, you cannot deduct the full year expenses. Only include the amounts spent for the months you had a qualified home office.

Example:

You started using the space in July when you purchased a desk and repainted your adult son's former bedroom (after he finally took all his belongs to his new apartment).

Record only the expenses from July through December on this form. You can choose to calculate by the month (6/12 x expense amount) or by the day (July 18 – December 31 = 166 days/365 = 45% of full-year amounts)

This ordinal day/date chart can help calculate number of days used:

http://www.atmos.anl.gov/ANLMET/OrdinalDa y.txt

Line 8: Enter the amount from Line 29 of Schedule C. This is your profit before taking any home office deduction. This is also the maximum amount you can deduct for any home office expenses. This figure will be used in calculations throughout this form.

On the plus side, if your home office expenses are greater than the amount on Line 8, you can carry the excess forward to additional years, when you may be more profitable, so you won't actually lose the deductions just because you had a slow year.

Line 9 Casualty losses is if you had theft or accident that was allowed as a Schedule A deduction. Unless your entire house was destroyed, the IRS rules for casualty losses rarely result in a deduction, so you can probably skip this one. If you filed Form 4684 for massive casualty losses, use the allowable deduction in the indirect column.

Line 10: Deductible mortgage interest on your home. Enter the total in the indirect column.

If you take the mortgage interest deduction here, you can only take a portion of the total amount on Schedule A.

Example:

Your house is 1500 square feet.

Home office 150 square feet.

= Office expenses are 10% of total expenses.

Mortgage interest is $10,000

You will deduct $1000 of mortgage interest here ($10,000 x 10%), allowing you only the remaining $9,000 of deductible mortgage interest on Schedule A.

You can't deduct the same portion of the expense twice.

Line 11 Real Estate Taxes: the same pro-rating rule applies here, so be sure to subtract the business portion out before filling in Schedule A.

Line 17: Homeowners or renter's insurance premiums go here.

Line 18: *Rent* you paid on the house or apartment. If you own the property you won't have anything here. Mortgage payments are not considered rent.

Line 19-24: self-explanatory

Line 25: Carryover from previous year form 8829. If on the last tax return you could not deduct some or all of your home office expenses due to profitability limitations (Line 8 amounts), you can carry forward the undeducted amount here. You will be able to keep bringing these amounts forward to deduct in more profitable years.

Example:

In 2012 you had profits of $3500, but home office expenses of $4000. Since you could not deduct the full $3500, you are allowed to carryover the $500 to future years.

Part III Depreciation

This can be a bit tricky, so again, if you have trouble with it, you should probably consult a professional tax preparer. I will give the general theory for you, but the calculations can become complex. Some tax prep software will do the heavy lifting for you. Or you can choose to use the simplified method for calculating the home office deduction.

The IRS instruction booklet for Form 8829 has a schedule of values to use on this form for calculating depreciation. I will not reproduce those figures here, but you can download the PDF instructions using this link:

http://www.irs.gov/pub/irs-pdf/i8829.pdf

You only claim depreciation on a home you own. If you rent a house or apartment, you do not get to claim depreciation; the owner of the property already claims it.

Depreciation is only calculated on the value of the structure (building) not on the land. If you don't have a good idea of the value of your home, use the appraised value on your real estate tax bill. Most bills break out the value of land and "improvements," which means buildings. If you made significant additional improvements to your home since the last appraisal, you can include those in the basis or value. What can and cannot be included is tricky (repairs cannot, but improvements can) so it's best to consult an expert on this, or go with the real estate tax appraisal.

Bottom line: document how you calculated the value of the house in your records.

The depreciation percentage is calculated as a percentage of the value, depending on when you first started using your home for business. If you have more than one business, then use the earliest date.

Total up all the expenses related to the house, then take the pro-rated portion on Line 35 and carry it over to Schedule C Line 30.

Depending on the value of your home and its age, you can see that depreciation alone might bring your Schedule C net profit to zero. This is why there is a limitation on how much you can deduct.

N.S. Smith & EM Lynley

Chapter 8: Self-Employment Tax

This is probably the topic that causes the most frustration for writers, and anyone else who's self-employed. When you have a regular job, your employer pays half of your social security and Medicare taxes for you, the other half gets withheld from your paycheck. You can see how much on your pay stub and W-2.

Self-employed people have to pay that employer portion too. Yes it sucks. But the IRS gives you a tax break as an adjustment to income and doesn't levy any income tax on the employer portion of this tax. Tax software will automatically calculate it and subtract it on Line 27 of Form 1040.

You'll have to pay SE tax if your net profit on Schedule C is more than $400. If you make $399, you owe no SE. If you make $400, you owe SE tax on all $400.

The top part of Schedule SE has a scary-looking flow chart that puts you in a bad mood before you even start filling anything out, but you can just ignore it, unless you work in the clergy. Otherwise, keep reading and I'll let you know which form you need to use.

If you use tax prep software, it will automatically choose the correct form for you, so don't worry. It is, however, a good idea to understand what's going on inside this form, because it isn't as bad as it appears at first, even if you owe SE tax.

There are two versions of Schedule SE, the long form and the short form. If you have another job that issues you a W-2, you must use the long form, because it calculates the amount of social security and

Medicare tax on your total earnings and takes into account any amounts withheld on a W-2.

If your spouse has a W-2 job and you do not, you can use the short form.

If the Schedule C earnings are all you got during the tax year, you can use the short form.

NOTE: If you and your spouse each have self-employment income, you will need to file separate Schedule SEs. The form is per individual, not per tax return, because social security and Medicare records are kept at the individual level, by social security number.

If you pay SE tax into the social security system, it has your name on it. It doesn't benefit your spouse at all. And your spouse's SS or Medicare withholding doesn't benefit you.

You'll need to finish your Schedule C before you can work form Schedule SE to calculate the amount of the tax on your profits. Carry that figure over to Form 1040, line 56. The rate comes to about 15 % (net to about 7% tax on the Schedule C net profit after you get the deduction for half of the SE tax on Line 27 of Form 1040.)

There's really no way to get around paying this tax. But as I mentioned earlier, SE tax allows you to count your self-employment income toward your eventual social security retirement benefits.

One thing to remember about SE tax: even if you have no taxable income on Line 38 (Adjusted Gross Income), you may still owe SE tax, since the SE tax threshold is much lower ($400) compared to the taxable income threshold. For writers who make only a modest profit, this can be a huge surprise.

The SE tax can also wreak havoc with your tax situation when you or your spouse also has a day job, since your federal income tax withholding doesn't take the writing income or SE tax into account. To be on the safe side, you should be estimating your writing/self-employment net profit situation quarterly and sending in the required payments to cover the additional taxes. This will be covered in detail in the next chapter.

My general advice to writers is to get a financial snapshot during early December so you can see how much SE tax you are likely to owe for the year. If you are correctly calculating and submitting your estimated tax payments, that should be easy.

If you are close to the $400 mark, consider moving up some of the following year's spending into December, to get you under $400.

If you are nowhere near $400, then you can't really affect SE tax much, so don't sweat it, but at least know how much more you're going to owe, so you don't get a big ugly surprise when you finally get around the Schedule C.

If you're reading this book at the beginning of the year, there's not much you can do now to affect SE tax for last year. But once you get a nasty April surprise, you'll probably be more diligent in keeping a running total of P/L.

Again, a reminder that avoiding SE tax isn't necessarily a smart goal, because it's going toward your retirement account. You'll want to look at the big picture of your financial situation to decide what's the best course for you to take.

Special SE Situations

If you have two separate businesses and file separate Schedule C for each (writing and formatting, or writing and editing), combine the net income or loss for all businesses when paying SE tax. The loss on one business will balance any net profit from the other business.

Example:

Frieda Formatter earns income from both writing and formatting other authors' self-published books. Her writing has lots of expenses and occasionally she has a loss, while formatting is always profitable.

Writing net loss on Schedule C:	($ 230)
Formatting net profit	$1200
Amount subject to SE tax	$ 970

If you and your spouse run the business together as a partnership (which files Form 1065 and gives you a K-1 instead of Schedule C), then you each file a Schedule SE for your individual portion of the partnership income, based on your share of ownership. You should each receive a different K-1 anyway, but the tax will be proportional.

Chapter 9: Quarterly Estimated Payments

This is the second most frustrating issue facing self-employed writers.

The IRS is intended to be a pay-as-you-go system, which is why your employer takes federal income tax withholding out of each paycheck instead of once a month or letting you wait till April to pay. The IRS actually expects all taxpayers to make payments along the way as you earn income.

It's a lot harder to do this when you're self-employed because earnings and expenses are not well-matched up. So the IRS devised the system of quarterly tax payments.

You may decide calculating estimated payments is too much hassle for you. That's fine. The IRS has decided that if your balance due in April is over $1000 they will assess you a 10% penalty for not planning better. So consider reevaluating your opinion of quarterly payments. How much is it worth to you to avoid a little recordkeeping and some simple math?

If you just can't come up with the amount owed in a particular quarter, pay *something,* even just $25, or the IRS assumes you're trying to get around the rules. If you are earning writing profits of over $10,000 or writing full time with no other income, the IRS is not going to accept an excuse that you were too busy or didn't realize you owed them anything before April 15.

How to Calculate Quarterly Taxes

The IRS has a handy publication and set of byzantine rules and worksheets to "help" you figure out how much tax you owe each quarter. Frankly, they confuse even me and there isn't any software set up to do this as far as I know.

I have developed my own system for calculating the quarterly payment that should keep you from the $1000 penalty mark even if it's not completely accurate.

Step 1: figure out what tax bracket you're in. If you use tax software, it reported your bracket in the summary section when you finished your return last year. If you don't have that figure here are the brackets for 2013:

Remember to add up your profit from your writing plus any wage or other income for yourself or spouse when determining your tax bracket.

If you have no clue how much profit you will make in 2014, then use your 2013 tax bracket results after you file your 2013 tax return. The brackets are so large, that unless you are close to the cutoff, it's not going to be difficult to guess your bracket.

Tax rate	Single	Married filing jointly or QW
10%	Up to $8,925	Up to $17,850
15%	$8,926 – 36,250	$17,851- $72,500
25%	Up to $87,850	Up to $146,400
28%	Up to $183,250	Up to $223,050
33%	$398,350	Up to $398,350
35%	$400,000	Up to $450,000
39.6%	over $400,001	Over $450,001

Tax rate	Married filing separately	Head of household
10%	Up to $8,925	Up to $12,750
15%	$8,926 – $36,250	$12,751 - $48,600
25%	Up to $73,200	Up to $125,450
28%	Up to $111,525	Up to $203,150
33%	Up to $199,175	Up to $398,350
35%	Up to $225,000	Up to $425,000
39.6%	Over $225,001	Over $425,001

Step 2: At the end of each quarter, calculate how much you earned from self-employment during that quarter.

Step 3: Subtract out all your expenses for the quarter. It won't be difficult if you've been keeping track at least once per month. Estimate the things you don't have precise information for.

Step 4: Calculate how much tax you would owe on the quarterly profit at your tax bracket rate, plus the 8 percent of SE tax (I round it up to 10 %).

NOTE: Do not include any day-job income when doing Steps 3 through 5. The income from W-2 jobs is only used to determine your tax bracket.

If you have other sources of income that do not have withholding, such as pensions, investments, etc., you may want to send in an additional amount just for the income tax levied in your tax bracket. This income is not subject to SE tax.

Example:

Wanda Writer earned $1500 in Q1 2014 and had $450 in expenses that quarter.

She's in the 15 % tax bracket when she takes into account other income she expects during the year.

Net SE earnings ($1500-450) = $1050

x 15 % tax bracket= 157.50

+ 10% of the profit = 105.00

Add that up: $262.50

Wanda should send it a Q1 2014estimated tax payment of $262.50to the IRS on Form ES by April 15, 2014.

Don't worry that it might get confused with your 2013 tax return or payment (also due on April 15, 2014). You'll be filing a special Estimated Tax form and indicating that this amount is for 2014 taxes.

If Wanda has a day job, this quarterly payment will get counted on top of the 2014 withholding and Wanda will report it as taxes already paid when she files her tax return for this tax year.

Example:

Wanda's day job at a day care center already withholds Federal income tax, Social Security and Medicare. When she gets her W-2, it shows $1350 of withholding for income tax in Box 2.

During the same tax year, Wanda sent in estimated tax payments of $625.

When Wanda files her tax return, she will record:

$1350 of federal withholding (on Line 62 of Form 1040)

$625 of estimated tax payments (Line 63 "estimated tax payments" on Form 1040)

$1975 total payments for the year

If her total tax due (including any SE tax) is less than $1975, she will get a refund for the overpayment, whether it was due to excess withholding or an incorrect estimate.

If she owes more than $1975, she will pay the IRS whatever balance is due.

Most writers' incomes fluctuate dramatically from quarter to quarter, so recalculate every quarter and send in the appropriate amount for the net profit year-to-date. It won't be exactly what you owe at the end of the day, but it will be close, and will help you avoid a big tax bill in April and the dreaded underpayment penalty.

Example

In Q1 and Q2 Wanda estimated profit of $1000 and $200 respectively, and sent in the correct amount of estimated tax for her tax bracket, $250 and $50, for a total of $300 sent in for Q1 and Q2.

In Q3 she had expenses of $1000 but no earnings. She doesn't owe any estimated taxes for Q3 because she had no net profit.

In Q4 she earned $1000, but had no expenses.

Does Wanda have to pay an estimated payment for Q4?

1. The easy answer is yes. She can calculate a Q4 tax payment of $250 on the $1000 net profit for that quarter. It's fine if she wants to do it this way, but she may be paying more than she needs to, since she isn't taking the Q3 loss into account

2. The more complicated answer will include the full year P and L picture to see how much she owes, taking into account the fluctuations.

The math may be a bit tricky unless you work with numbers a lot.

Full year P & L

Q1	$1000
Q2	$200
Q3	($1000)
Q4	$1000

Total estimated profit = $1200

Wanda's estimated tax payments on $1200 (15% tax bracket x 1200 + 10 % SE tax x 1200)

= $300

Estimated tax paid to date = $300

RESULT: Wanda doesn't actually need to send in any more estimated payments based on the year-to-date net profit estimates.

Of course, to be on the safe side, if you think you might have underestimated earnings, go ahead and send in a little bit now.

If you underestimated your expenses during the year (very likely if you haven't been keeping perfect records during the year), when you file Schedule C in April chances are high you'll owe less and can get a refund.

If you've been keeping meticulous track of your expenses all year, you will have less paper chasing to do when you file the return. If not, you'll have to fill in a lot of missing information to file an accurate tax return and take all the deductions you deserve.

Recap:

1. Calculate net profits every quarter

2. Calculate SE tax due for that quarter

3. Calculate year-to-date net profits and SE tax on that amount

4. Pay the difference if your year-to-date SE tax owed is more than you have already paid so far. If you have overpaid due to

a negative quarter, it will get resolved either in the next quarter's payment or when you file the return.

When to File Estimated Taxes

For estimated tax purposes, the year is divided into four payment periods. Each period has a specific payment due date. If you do not pay enough tax by the due date of each of the payment periods, you may be charged a penalty even if you are due a refund when you file your income tax return.

If you don't have a profit in a particular quarter, you can skip the payment for that quarter.

For the period:	Due date:
Jan. 1 – March 31	April 15
April 1 – May 31	June 15
June 1 – August 31	September 15
Sept. 1 – Dec. 31	January 15 next year. If you file your return by January 15, you do not have to pay the estimate for Q4

Where to Get Estimated Tax Forms

Send in your payment (check or money order) with a payment voucher from Form 1040-ES. Download the form from IRS.gov:

Follow the directions on how to mark your check or the payment may not get credited properly.

http://www.irs.gov/pub/irs-pdf/f1040es.pdf

Chapter 10: Unpublished Authors

Many businesses incur costs before they even have any revenue to show for their efforts. Think of a restaurant. It takes plenty of money to renovate and furnish, hire chefs and order food, before even one appetizer or cocktail gets served.

Why can't writers follow this example?

We can.

If you've been writing your novel for four years and have 100 pages done, I don't recommend calling yourself a writing business and filling up your Schedule C with a lot of expenses like a new desk, computer and, ten writing courses at the local college. You may be a writer, but you aren't yet to the point of having a writing *business*.

However, if you've finished at least one work and have made a serious effort to get it published, you're in business. Rejection is part of the game. Keep a spreadsheet of what you've written, which publishers or agents you've sent it to, and their response. (You should be doing this anyway, but you probably didn't think the IRS would care. They do.)

Those rejection letters/emails are proof you tried to make sales.

If you've gotten a manuscript accepted at a publisher but it hasn't released yet, you are definitely in business. Don't be afraid to keep track of your expenses and file that Schedule C for 2013, even if you won't start seeing revenues until 2014. You won't be able to write that stuff off next on your 2014 return when you do have income from writing, so do it now. If you can front-load some expenses, you will have fewer on next year's return, and that can help you make a profit. Remember, to avoid being investigated as a hobby (discussed in Chapter 2) you'll need to show profit in 3 out of every 5 years.

Example:

Billy Bob Biographer wrote a book on the life George Washington's dentist (remember those wooden teeth?). He finished it in July of 2013 and submitted it to 129 publishers during August and September. He got 128 rejection letters and one acceptance in October 2013 His book is scheduled to be released in January 2014.

Billy Bob did not earn anything in 2013, but he sold a manuscript. (No advance, sorry, Billy Bob). His first writing income will be reported during 2014, assuming someone buys it. But he did have some expenses during the writing of the book. He can legally file a Schedule C for 2013, even with no income, to report the expenses he had during 2013. Because writers use the cash method, he isn't allowed to count his income before he gets it, or delay recording his expenses until he has income.

Why would you want to start out your business with a loss? Why not wait till you have some income?

Because as I mentioned in Chapter 2, if you have other income from your day job, investments, etc., (not on a Schedule C), a loss on the Schedule C will lower your taxable income. That means you pay less tax. That's a good thing.

The IRS doesn't like to see people using Schedule C sideline businesses just for the purpose of lowering income, so if next year you earn both writing revenue and (hopefully) a profit, they won't question it. They only start poking into your situation when you have large and regular Schedule C losses that make a substantial dent in your regular wage income. They'll suspect your writing is a hobby and not a business, which is why they set up that profit in three out of five years rule.

So, as long as you keep records of your expenses, document and explain any expenditures and don't attempt to write off ridiculous amounts, the IRS won't even question you. If they do, you simply produce your receipts for expenses, your rejection letters and that one acceptance.

If your book is scheduled for release near the beginning of the year, you may even have advertising and promotional expenses in the prior tax year. That's okay. It's going to pay off once the book is released. Again, document each expense, including which book title it's for.

12/20 Facebook ads $15.00

(Pre-release promo for *How to Make Money Painting Rocks*)

Publisher's advances

If you are lucky enough to write for a publisher that pays advances, you will indeed have writing income well before you have sales. You may never earn out your advance, but that doesn't matter when it comes to taxes.

You could at some point even find yourself in a situation with an advance in one tax year, and a release the following year which never pays additional royalties. This is the opposite of the new writer with expenses and no income in a year.

To keep the IRS from getting suspicious about your dedication to writing as a business, make sure a good chunk of your expenditures in the year of the book release are for ads and promotion. You must be seen to be trying to sell the book.

Chapter 11: Self-Published Authors

We've already touched on a number of issues for self-published authors in previous sections, but I will go over the main topics again here, and encourage you to go back and read the relevant sections carefully to understand the specifics.

Self-published authors are writers *and* publishers. For this reason, you will have a set of expenses different from the average author who works with a publishers. You will most likely be paying other individual for services, like editing, formatting, and cover art.

- Make sure to get an EIN or Employer ID number, even if you don't expect to hire any employees. You may have already noticed the need to give a tax ID number to your distributors in order to get paid. If you don't have an EIN, you have to give your Social Security Number (SSN) which leaves you vulnerable to identity theft. There's nothing anyone can do with your EIN that would mess you up. They can't even file a tax return with it, since unless you are incorporated, you would need your SSN to file anyway.

- Require a W-9 or W8-BEN from everyone you pay, *before* you pay them. Having these forms on file absolves you from the obligation to withhold a portion of your payment for anyone who has a US tax obligation.

  a. W-9 for US citizens

  b. W8-BEN for people in other countries

      c. It DOES NOT matter whether the recipient has to pay tax or report the income. The onus is on you to keep accurate paperwork for the IRS on your expenses, even if the other person uses it to start a fire in their fireplace. Follow the rules and requirements that pertain to *your* business, and you'll be in good shape.

- Keep careful records of who you pay during the year. Even though the IRS requires you to furnish a 1099-MISC only for payments over $600 to any one individual, consider sending them to each independent contractor you use. This makes you look more like a business, and the IRS likes having more, rather than less, paperwork on your business activities.

      a. Again, the requirement is on you to report this expense, even if the recipient does not report the income on their own return, or even file a return.

      b. If the person is outside of the US, only a filled-in W8-BEN relieves you of the obligation to file the 1099-MISC. Protect yourself with the correct paperwork.

- Send 1099-MISC to all US independent contractors by January 31 following the end of the tax year. A copy of the forms should go to the IRS by the end of February.

- Set up separate checking, savings and credit card accounts for your writing/publishing business. Even if you have only a PayPal account, and funnel all payment through that account first, it's better than getting paid directly into your personal account. The IRS won't questions whether you are using business funds to pay for personal expenses you later write off as business expenses.

a. If you need the income from your business for your daily expenses, simply send it to your personal account as soon as it arrives in the PayPal account. (That's how I do it).

b. You can set up a free Ally bank account online for any distributors or publishers who don't work through PayPal. Amazon makes direct deposits, and this is a good way to keep that money separate at least as income, even if you don't keep it in the business account for very long.

- Don't forget the quarterly estimated tax payments.

- Because you are getting payments from many sources, rather than just one or two publishers, and paying out to many others, your bookkeeping is going to be more complicated.

    a. Set up a recordkeeping system you can work with easily and consistently. If you make it too detailed and complicated, you'll avoid using it, and find you are behind in both recording income/expenses, paying others and knowing your P/L situation in time to make the quarterly payment.

- Set up a calendar alert system to remind you to enter royalty information every month or quarter, and to calculate your quarterly taxes in enough time to make the payment schedule. If you are late, you may get a penalty and interest charge from the IRS.

    a. Penalties and interest on late quarterly payments or a balance due of over $1000 on self-employment tax show up in a letter the IRS sends you after you've filed your return.

b. Even if you get a refund at the end of the year, you may still incur a penalty for a later mid-year payment. The IRS gets paid by keeping a portion of your refund after you file your return. They follow up with a letter explaining how the amount was calculated. The more you earn, the more likely they will come after you for late or missing payments.

c. If you don't owe tax for a particular quarter, say Q3, consider sending in a payment anyway, knowing you'll be selling a lot during Q4. If you've overpaid, you will get the extra back when you file your final return for the year.

- If you receive royalties on behalf of another author and the amount is included on a 1099-MISC issued to you, you do not have to pay tax on this amount if you record the income and expense properly.

    a. Include the amount in your gross revenues/income.

    b. Deduct the amount on Line 10 (Commissions and fees).

Example: Joe Schmoe and a group of 9 other authors self-pubbed an anthology of car-mechanic romances. Joe pubbed the antho under his distributor accounts and got the payments. Every quarter he sent on the money due his collaborators. The antho earned $5,000 during 2013. Each author's portion was $500.

Joe received a total of $5,000 for this project on various distributor 1099-

MISCs during 2013. He includes the full amount in his 2013 income on Line 1 of his Schedule C.

He makes a 1099-MISC for each other author for their amounts paid during the tax year ($4,500), and deducts this on Line 10. He has no only included $500 of income on his own Schedule C for this project.

N.S. Smith & EM Lynley

FAQ

Can I write off a charitable donation from my business?

Unfortunately, the IRS does not allow Schedule C sole-proprietors to deduct charitable contribution made by their businesses. You can only write off these contributions as personal deductions on Schedule A, if you itemize.

Cash contributions by businesses are not allowed, only the value of goods you donate from your inventory.

If you donate a copy of a book, subtract it out of your inventory, and you'll essentially be able to write off the cost of the book. That's the only type of contribution you can legally deduct.

If I claim my home office expenses, will that affect my taxes when I sell my house?

Maybe.

If you use the new simplified method, you won't need to worry about depreciation.

If you use the old method, the depreciation you write off as home office expense must be subtracted from your home's basis when you sell the property. At the moment, up to $250,000 of capital gain on the sale of your residence ($500,000 for married couples) is excluded from taxes when you sell. But if that depreciation pushes your capital gain above the level of the exclusion, you may end up paying tax on some portion of the gains.

If you home is valued under $500,000, you won't have to worry about this, but for high-priced homes, it may become an issue. Just be aware of this when you sell the property and be sure to include the amount when calculating adjusted basis.

How long should I keep records?

While the IRS generally does not audit returns filed more than 3 years prior, they have the legal right to reexamine any prior year tax return. This is more likely if they find something suspicious and decide to take a second look at additional earlier years to see if the taxpayer made the same error in other years. To be on the safe side, keep business records for at least five years.

What if I didn't earn much at my writing business?

Any profit over $400 is subject to self-employment tax even if it's not subject to income tax (they are two separate things). So if you had a profit of less than $400 you won't owe SE tax, but you may still want to file Schedule C on your tax return. This will establish your profitability and avoid the hobby-loss rule from kicking in if you have losses in other tax years.

If you use Schedule C and deduct all the allowable expenses, you might find you've had a loss at writing for the year. You may want to use this to reduce your taxable income from other sources.

What do I do about state sales tax?

If your state collects sales tax and you sell print or e-books directly to customers in your state, you are required to collect tax and forward it to your state's sales tax agency. Visit your state's website for specific requirements, licenses and forms or call the agency for additional help. You can deduct the amount of sales tax forwarded to the state if you included it in your gross receipts/revenue figures.

I went to a writers' conference and my family came along. What can I deduct?

I received a question online about this and it's worth discussing in detail since the IRS is very particular about separating business from personal expenses.

Only the writer's travel expenses can be deducted on Schedule C.

- your airfare
- a pro-rated portion of accommodations, car rental, etc.
- your food. This is easiest if you calculate the pro-rated portion.

Example:

Wanda Writer, her husband and two kids go to Hawaii for the Sun and Sand Writers' Conference. They all stayed in the same hotel room. The hotel bill was $2,000. $150 of that was for kids' movies and room service for the kids and her husband.

She and her co-author rented a car and drove to a site at the other end of the island as research for a book they are writing together. Wanda had all her meals with the conference attendees except a $200 romantic dinner with her husband while another author babysat the kids.

Wanda can deduct:

- her conference registration fees
- her airfare
- $463 of the hotel charges (25% of the $1850 hotel bill after subtracting the kids' expenses)
- any meals she ate with the conference attendees (50% of the amount spent for items not provided by the conference)
- half the cost of the rental car and gasoline for the research trip with her co-author
- a portion of tips. (You have some leeway here. Deduct what you would have spent if you traveled alone. If you tipped the maid extra because your kids made a mess in the room, the extra is not a legitimate business expense).

Wanda cannot deduct:
- airfare for the rest of the family
- hotel charges for the rest of the family
- meals taken with the family
- babysitting charges

I didn't deduct something you mentioned when I filed a return for an earlier year. What can I do?

If the additional deduction changes the amount of taxable income and changes your balance due or refund, you can file an amended tax return for the year in question. You can file up to three years after the date the original return was due. For example, amendments to 2009 returns can be filed through April 15, 2013. 2010 amendments can be filed through April 15, 2014.

If the change does not result in a different tax liability, you do not need to file an amended return.

File Form 1040X for the specific year. You can get old tax forms on the IRS website:

Prior Year Forms

Ask a Question

Got a question I haven't addressed here? Send me an email. I'll try my best to answer it or provide the appropriate resource, and will add it in the next edition of this book.

Ask a question at my blog **Tax Tips for Authors:** (http://taxtips.emlynley.com or http://www.facebook.com/taxtipsforauthors).

However, I cannot legally or ethically offer specific tax advice based on an email. I can clarify any content in this book which is unclear. I am available to hire for consultation on your specific tax situation.

Thank you for buying this book and I hope it's been helpful for you.

N.S. Smith & EM Lynley

Where to Get Tax Forms

I've provided links to most of the forms you will need to do your business return if you are a sole proprietor filing a Schedule C. Here is a recap of the forms.

Schedule C

Form: http://www.irs.gov/pub/irs-pdf/f1040sc.pdf
Instructions: http://www.irs.gov/pub/irs-pdf/i1040sc.pdf

1099-MISC
Form: http://www.irs.gov/pub/irs-pdf/f1099msc.pdf
Instructions: http://www.irs.gov/pub/irs-pdf/i1099msc.pdf

Form 8829 Business Use of Home
Form: http://www.irs.gov/pub/irs-pdf/f8829.pdf
Instructions: http://www.irs.gov/pub/irs-pdf/i8829.pdf

While you may want to prepare you forms by hand, I suggest using tax prep software, or hiring a tax professional. New authors, or newly self-published authors dealing with a variety of unfamiliar issues should consider having a tax professional prepare their first return to make sure you get started on the right foot, rather than

Forms and Publications are available in PDF, and many of the forms allow you to input data in Adobe Acrobat and save it.

You can find additional forms at the IRS website. The Forms and Publications section allows you to search the name or number of any form and publication, including key word searches.

IRS Forms and Publications Page:
http://www.irs.gov/Forms-&-Pubs

About the Authors

N.S. SMITH holds the M.Sc. in Financial Economics from the London School of Economics and served as a staff economist in the White House Council of Economic Advisers. Under a pseudonym she has published more than twenty-five works of fiction.

EM LYNLEY writes erotic romance. She is a Rainbow Award winner, an EPPIE finalist, and writes for several different publishers. She also runs Smooth Draft Editing and loves to coach new writers. Visit her online:

Author Website: http://www.emlynley.com

Smooth Draft Editing: http://www.smoothdraft.com

Facebook: https://www.facebook.com/pages/Author-EM-Lynley/146199905400403

Tax Tips for Authors on Facebook:

http://www.facebook.com/taxtipsforauthors

N.S. Smith & EM Lynley

Other Titles by EM Lynley

NOVELS
Jaded
An Intoxicating Crush
Lighting the Way Home
Hostile Takeover
Italian Ice
Rarer Than Rubies
Sex, Lies & Wedding Bells
Bound for Trouble (Forthcoming Summer 2014)
Out of the Gate (Forthcoming Spring 2014)

NOVELLAS
Gingerbread Palace
Venus Envy
A Lesser Evil
Brand New Flavor
A Christmas Bonus

NON-FICTION
Tax Tips for Authors
How to Be a NaNoWriMo Winner
How to Revise Your NaNoWriMo Novel (forthcoming 2014)

EDITOR
Bedknobs & Beanstalks
Going for Gold Olympic Anthology
Wicked Good
Rumpled Silk Sheets

www.ingramcontent.com/pod-product-compliance
Lightning Source LLC
Chambersburg PA
CBHW022044190326
41520CB00008B/698